EROSION

EARLY BIRD EARTH SCIENCE

BY JOELLE RILEY

LERNER PUBLICATIONS COMPANY • MINNEAPOLIS

The images in this book are used with permission of: © Michael S. Sutton, pp. 1, 6 (background), 10 (background), 25 (background), 30 (background), 36 (background), 44 (background), 45 (background), 46 (background), 47 (background); © PhotoDisc Royalty Free by Getty Images, p. 1 (title type); © National Park Service, pp. 4, 5, 8, 9, 13, 16, 22, 25, 27, 35, 43, 46, 47, 48 (both); © U.S. Geological Survey Photo Library, p. 6; NASA, p. 7; © Marli Miller/Visuals Unlimited, pp. 10, 11, 29; © Cherie Winner, pp. 12, 14, 20, 38; © Mark Gibson/Visuals Unlimited, p .15; © Todd Strand/Independent Picture Service, pp. 17, 21 (both); © Joe Mastroianni/National Science Foundation, p. 18; © Kristan Hutchison/National Science Foundation, p. 19; © W. Cody/CORBIS, p. 23; © Gerald & Buff Corsi/Visuals Unlimited, pp. 24, 28; © Adam Jones/Visuals Unlimited, pp. 26, 41; © Clint Farlinger/Visuals Unlimited, p. 30; © Science VU/GSFC/Visuals Unlimited, p. 32; © David B. Fleetham/Visuals Unlimited, p. 33; © Boyle & Boyle/Animals Animals, p. 34; © Ed Darack/Visuals Unlimited, p. 36; © Science VU-ARS/Visuals Unlimited, p. 37; © James McCullagh/Visuals Unlimited, p. 39; © Jerome Wexler/Visuals Unlimited, p. 42.

Front Cover: © Paul A. Souders/CORBIS.
Front Cover Title Type: © PhotoDisc Royalty Free by Getty Images.
Back Cover: © Reuters/CORBIS.

Illustrations on pp. 31, 40 by Laura Westlund, copyright © by Lerner Publications Company.

Lerner Publications Company
A division of Lerner Publishing Group
241 First Avenue North
Minneapolis, MN 55401 U.S.A.

Website address: www.lernerbooks.com

Library of Congress Cataloging-in-Publication Data

Riley, Joelle.
    Erosion / by Joelle Riley.
        p.   cm. — (Early bird Earth science)
    Includes index.
    ISBN-13: 978–0–8225–5949–8 (lib. bdg. : alk. paper)
    ISBN-10: 0–8225–5949–8 (lib. bdg. : alk. paper)
        1. Erosion—Juvenile literature. 2. Nature—Effect of human beings on—Juvenile literature.
3. Children and the environment—Juvenile literature. I. Title. II. Series.
    QE571.R55 2007
    551.3'02—dc22   2005024476

Manufactured in the United States of America
1 2 3 4 5 6 – JR – 12 11 10 09 08 07

CONTENTS

BE A WORD DETECTIVE

Can you find these words as you read about erosion? Be a detective and try to figure out what they mean. You can turn to the glossary on page 46 for help.

canyon   erosion   moraine

cave   glacier   mouth

delta   meanders   plow

deposition   minerals   weathering

dune

CHAPTER 1
THE CHANGING EARTH

Earth is changing all the time. Some changes happen quickly. In moments, an earthquake can move large amounts of rock and soil. Other changes happen slowly. It takes many years for a mountain to form.

6

Erosion (uh-ROH-zhuhn) is the movement of rock, soil, and other bits of earth. Erosion happens everywhere on the planet. It usually happens very slowly. But over time, erosion makes big changes in the land.

Erosion helps to change the land's shape everywhere on the planet.

Erosion changes the shapes of tall mountains. The mountains in the eastern United States are old. Once they were tall and had sharp tops. But over thousands of years, erosion wore them down. The mountains are not as tall as they once were. Their peaks have become rounded and smooth. And erosion is still at work. It is making the mountains smaller and smaller.

The Appalachian Mountains are in the eastern United States. They are old and have rounded tops.

The Rocky Mountains are in the western United States. They are young and have pointed tops.

The mountains of the western United States are young. They have tall, pointed tops. But erosion is slowly changing them. In many years, these mountains will be worn down too.

Rock from this mountain has broken into small pieces. What can cause rock to break?

CHAPTER 2
BREAKING UP THE GROUND

Big pieces of earth are harder to move than small pieces. Erosion can't move a whole mountain at once. But it can move pieces that have broken off a mountain. Erosion can move rocks and bits of soil. Making large pieces of earth into smaller pieces is called weathering. Water, ice, and growing plants all cause weathering.

Hard rain on a mountain causes weathering.

During a heavy rain, water pounds down. Big raindrops hit the ground. The raindrops break off pieces of earth. Some of the rainwater soaks into the soil. The rest of the water runs across the ground. As the water flows, it rubs against the ground. The flowing water breaks off more small pieces of earth.

The rain pounds on the ground. It breaks off little bits of earth.

This stream flows very fast. It can break loose a lot of rock and soil.

The water in rivers and streams rubs against the ground too. As a stream flows, pieces of soil and rock break loose. Fast streams push harder than slow streams. So fast streams break away more earth than slow streams.

Soft earth weathers quickly. A stream flowing over soft ground spreads out. It becomes shallow and wide. The stream meanders (mee-AN-derz) across the ground. It bends from side to side in big loops.

This stream bends back and forth. It is meandering.

This is a picture of a canyon. The stream flowing at the bottom created the canyon.

Hard rock weathers very slowly. Streams flowing across hard rock don't usually spread out or meander. Instead, they follow a narrow, straight path. As a stream flows, it rubs against the rock. The stream digs deeper and deeper into the rock. After a very long time, a canyon forms. A canyon is a deep, narrow valley with steep sides.

The water in lakes and oceans doesn't flow across the land. But it moves back and forth in waves. The waves pound against the shore. They break loose bits of rock, sand, and soil.

Pounding waves cause weathering of rock and soil.

These bottles started out with the same amount of water. Then one bottle was frozen. The water changed to ice. You can see that the ice takes up more space than the water does.

Water also causes weathering when it freezes. Rainwater soaks into tiny cracks in the ground and in rocks. If the weather is cold enough, the water freezes. It becomes ice. Ice takes up more space than water does. So as water changes into ice, it gets bigger. It pushes against the soil and rocks. It makes the tiny cracks bigger. Pieces of soil and rock break loose.

A slowly moving sheet of ice is called a glacier (GLAY-sher). Glaciers form in places that stay cold most of the time. When snow falls in these places, it doesn't melt. Instead, the snow just piles up. As the snow gets deeper, it packs tightly together. It becomes a thick sheet of ice. It is now a glacier.

A glacier is a huge, slowly moving sheet of ice.

Glaciers carry rocks and soil with them as they flow.

The glacier flows downhill very slowly. It grinds against the ground as it moves. It breaks off chunks of soil and rock.

Plants are growing in cracks in this rock. The plants' roots push against the rock. The pushing makes the cracks grow bigger.

Plants can cause weathering too. Most plants grow in soil. But sometimes plants grow on rock. The plants' roots grow down into cracks in the rock. The roots push against the rock. They push so hard that they make the cracks bigger.

Chemicals (KEM-uh-kuhlz) and other substances can also cause weathering. Some chemicals can dissolve rock the way water dissolves sugar. Tiny bits of rock come loose and mix with the chemicals. Other substances change rock in other ways.

Water falls on a pile of sugar. The water dissolves the sugar. Water can dissolve some kinds of rock too.

Chemicals found in rainwater can dissolve a kind of rock called limestone. When the limestone dissolves, a space is left where the limestone used to be. If enough limestone dissolves, a cave forms. A cave is a hole under the ground.

This cave is made of a kind of rock called limestone. The cave formed when water dissolved some of the limestone.

This rock has a lot of iron in it. The rock is orange because the iron has turned into rust.

Other chemicals change rock so that it breaks more easily. Some kinds of rock contain a metal called iron. Air and water can change the iron in rock into rust. Rust is not as strong as iron. The rock breaks more easily.

Sometimes weathering happens quickly. Sometimes it happens slowly. Soil is softer than rock. It breaks up more easily than rock. So soil weathers faster than rock. And softer rock weathers faster than harder rock.

This kind of rock called sandstone is soft. It breaks apart very easily.

Weathering has broken up the rocks on this hillside. What happens after weathering makes bits of soil and rock?

CHAPTER 3

MOVING THE PIECES

Erosion happens after soil and rock have been broken down by weathering. Most erosion is caused by water, ice, and wind.

Moving water carries bits of soil and rock with it. Water that moves quickly pushes harder than water that moves slowly. So water that moves quickly can carry bigger pieces of earth than water that moves slowly.

Fast-moving water can carry big pieces of earth just as it can carry boats down a river.

Waves pick up sand from this beach.

Rain flowing across the ground picks up tiny bits of soil. Streams and rivers pick up soil and rocks. Waves pick up soil, sand, and stones from the shores of lakes and oceans.

Glaciers pick up soil and rocks as they flow along the ground. Glaciers are very hard and very heavy. They push hard against the ground. They push so hard that they can carry huge rocks.

A flowing glacier can carry big rocks.

Bits of dust are very light. Wind can lift them high off the ground.

Wind blows across the ground and moves pieces of earth. It pushes heavier bits along the ground. Lighter bits are lifted high into the air. Strong winds can pick up large amounts of sand, dust, and soil.

This stream is carrying a lot of soil. It will drop off the soil in a new place. What is this called?

CHAPTER 4
BUILDING NEW LAND

Soil, rocks, and sand are carried away by erosion. But they don't just disappear. They are dropped off in new places. This is called deposition (DEP-uh-ZIH-shuhn).

Moving water can carry bits of earth.
But sooner or later the water slows down or
stops moving. Then the soil and rocks fall to
the bottom.

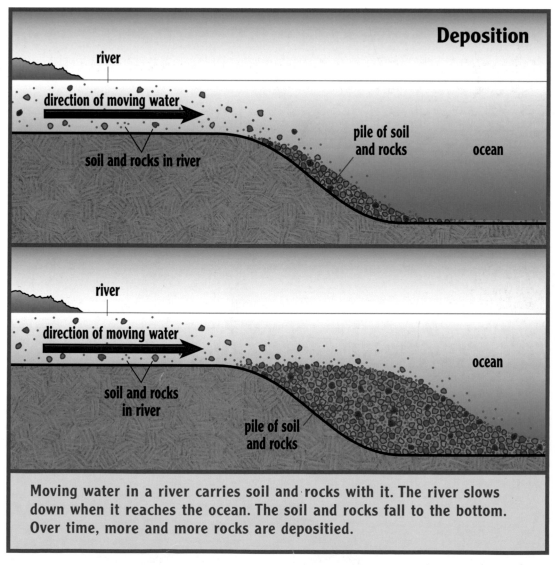

Deposition

river

direction of moving water

soil and rocks in river

pile of soil
and rocks

ocean

river

direction of moving water

soil and rocks
in river

pile of soil
and rocks

ocean

Moving water in a river carries soil and rocks with it. The river slows
down when it reaches the ocean. The soil and rocks fall to the bottom.
Over time, more and more rocks are depositied.

A lot of earth is deposited at a river's mouth. The mouth is the place where the river flows into a lake or ocean. At the river's mouth, the water slows down and spreads out. The river deposits soil and rocks in a fan shape called a delta.

This picture was taken from the sky. It shows a river's delta.

This beach is made of sand, small stones, and seashells.

The ocean deposits bits of earth too. Ocean waves slow down as they reach the land. The waves deposit sand, small stones, and seashells along the shore. Over time, the sand, stones, and shells pile up to form a beach.

This hill was made by a glacier. It is called a moraine (mor-AYN).

As glaciers slide downhill, they may move into a place that is warmer. Then the front of the glacier melts. When the ice melts, the soil and rocks in it are deposited on the ground. The soil may pile up to make a hill. A hill made by a glacier is called a moraine.

When wind slows down, it deposits the dust or sand that it was carrying. In some areas, the wind blows in the same direction year after year. And it always slows down at the same place. Dust and sand pile up in this place. After a while, a hill forms. A hill made out of sand is called a dune.

These huge dunes are made of sand.

People do many things that change the land. Why is soil blowing away as this tractor drives across a field?

CHAPTER 5
EROSION AND PEOPLE

Water, ice, and wind are not the only things that cause erosion. People cause erosion too.

Farmers plow fields to plant seeds. When they plow, they make grooves in the soil. Plowing loosens the soil. Wind can blow the loose soil away. If the farmer plows up and down hills, rainwater can run downhill through the grooves. The moving water can carry the soil away.

Some of the soil in this cornfield has washed away.

People cut down many trees. Trees protect the ground from erosion. A tree's roots hold on to the soil. The roots keep soil from washing away or blowing away. And a tree's branches and leaves keep rain from pounding against the ground. When trees are cut down, the soil can be washed or blown away.

Plant roots and tree roots hold soil in place. They keep the soil from eroding.

Once there was land in front of these houses. Water has carried most of it away. If more land erodes, the houses may fall down.

Soil is important. Most plants need soil to grow in. And soil is part of the ground that we build houses on. If too much soil is eroded, plants may die. If a very large amount of soil is washed down a hill, it may carry whole houses with it!

A farmer's plow digs grooves in the ground for planting seeds. If the grooves go from the top to the bottom of a hill, rain can run down the hill, carrying soil with it.

If the grooves go along the side of the hill, they catch the rain. The grooves keep the rain from carrying soil down the hill.

People can do things to protect the soil. Farmers can plow their fields so that the grooves follow the sides of hills. If rainwater can't run downhill, it can't carry soil away. People can grow plants on hillsides. The plants' roots keep rain from washing away the soil. People can also plant rows of trees or bushes near open fields. A row of trees or bushes blocks the wind. It keeps strong winds from blowing soil away.

Trees help protect this field from wind erosion.

Good soil will help this plant grow.

Some erosion helps people. People grow plants for food. The plants need good soil to grow. The soil has to have minerals (MIN-ur-uhlz) in it. Minerals in the soil come from tiny bits of rock. Erosion breaks rocks into the tiny bits that help plants grow.

Erosion is happening all the time. Rock and soil are being weathered. Bits of dirt are being moved around. Big mountains are being worn down. Earth is always changing.

Over many years, erosion will change the shape of these mountains. They will become smoother and smoother.

ON SHARING A BOOK

When you share a book with a child, you show that reading is important. To get the most out of the experience, read in a comfortable, quiet place. Turn off the television and limit other distractions, such as telephone calls. Be prepared to start slowly. Take turns reading parts of this book. Stop occasionally and discuss what you're reading. Talk about the photographs. If the child begins to lose interest, stop reading. When you pick up the book again, revisit the parts you have already read.

BE A VOCABULARY DETECTIVE

The word list on page 5 contains words that are important in understanding the topic of this book. Be word detectives and search for the words as you read the book together. Talk about what the words mean and how they are used in the sentence. Do any of these words have more than one meaning? You will find the words defined in a glossary on page 46.

WHAT ABOUT QUESTIONS?

Use questions to make sure the child understands the information in this book. Here are some suggestions:

> What did this paragraph tell us? What does this picture show? What do you think we'll learn about next? What is a delta? What causes weathering? What do people do to cause erosion? What is your favorite part of the book? Why?

If the child has questions, don't hesitate to respond with questions of your own, such as What do *you* think? Why? What is it that you don't know? If the child can't remember certain facts, turn to the index.

INTRODUCING THE INDEX

The index helps readers find information without searching through the whole book. Turn to the index on page 48. Choose an entry such as *wind* and ask the child to use the index to find out how wind plays a part in erosion. Repeat with as many entries as you like. Ask the child to point out the differences between an index and a glossary. (The index helps readers find information, while the glossary tells readers what words mean.)

EROSION

BOOKS

Coombs, Karen Mueller. *Children of the Dust Days.* **Minneapolis: Carolrhoda Books, Inc., 2000.** Learn about the Dust Bowl Era in the United States through the eyes of children.

Hooper, Meredith. *The Pebble in My Pocket: A History of Our Earth.* **New York: Viking**, 1996. When a young girl finds a pebble, she wonders where it came from. To find the answer to this question, she learns about Earth's history.

Rutten, Joshua. *Erosion.* **Chanhassen, MN: The Child's World, 1999.** This book gives basic facts about soil and erosion.

Planet Earth. **Alexandria, VA: Time-Life Books, 1997.** Read all about our planet.

Winner, Cherie. *Erosion.* **Minneapolis: Carolrhoda Books, Inc., 1999.** Text and color photos tell about erosion in different parts of the United States.

WEBSITES

How Rocks Are Formed
http://www.rocksforkids.com/RFK/howrocks.html
This site explains how rocks form and includes information about erosion.

National Park Service
http://www.nps.gov
The National Park Service has information about parks all across the United States. You can find out if there is a national park near your home. You can find examples of erosion at many of these parks.

The Virtual Cave
http://www.goodearthgraphics.com/virtcave/erosional_caves/erosional.html
This website has photos of caves formed by erosion.

GLOSSARY

canyon: a deep, narrow valley with very steep sides

cave: a hole under the ground

delta: a fan-shaped area made of soil and rocks deposited at the mouth of a river

deposition (DEP-uh-ZIH-shuhn): dropping off soil, rocks, and sand that were carried away by erosion

dune: a hill made out of sand

erosion (uh-ROH-zhuhn): the movement of rock, soil, and other bits of earth. Erosion is caused by water, ice, and wind.

glacier (GLAY-sher): a thick sheet of ice that moves across the land

meanders (mee-AN-derz): bends from side to side in big loops. Streams that flow over soft ground usually meander.

minerals (MIN-ur-uhlz): substances found in nauture. Minerals are solid. They are not alive.

moraine (mor-AYN): a hill made by a glacier

mouth: the place where a river flows into a lake or ocean

plow: to make grooves in the soil to plant seeds

weathering: making rocks and soil into smaller pieces.
Weathering is caused by water, ice, and growing plants.

INDEX

Pages listed in **bold** type refer to photographs.